Filthy Franny and the 4 Faery Fleas

BY M.W. PENN
& MIKE LINTON

Vancouver, BC
gumboot books
www.gumbootbooks.com

"For Eileen Spinelli,
who inspires poets and dreamers.
With gratitude and love."
M.W.P.

"For my darling Izuniu.
My never ending source
of inspiration and motivation."
M.L.

This book was printed in the USA on acid free paper that contains no fibre from old growth forests, using ink that is safe for children.

poetry © 2009 by M.W. Penn
artwork © 2009 by Mike Linton

Filthy Franny and the 4 Faery Fleas first published in Canada in 2009 by Gumboot Books.

All rights reserved.

No part of this book may be reproduced in any form or by any means, electronic or mechanical, including photocopying and recording, or by any information storage and retrieval system without permission in writing from the publisher.
www.gumbootbooks.com

ISBN 978-0-9784351-6-5

Note for Librarians

A cataloguing record for this title is available from Library and Archives Canada at:

www.collectionscanada.ca/amicus/index-e.html

Filthy Franny never washed!
Her parents gave up hope
of ever teaching Franny
how to use a bar of soap.
And though they often said to her,
"You're dirty, little daughter,"
they couldn't get dear Franny
to go near a tub of water.

Filthy Franny had no friends:
no children would come near her.
She had to yell quite loudly
to have other children hear her
across the open spaces
that they had to keep between
themselves and filthy Franny
if they wanted to stay clean.

So Franny would play all alone
and dream of going places
with cakes and kings and wondrous things
like moons with purple faces.

"Now if I were a lucky kid –
like Cinderella say –
I'd have a Faery Godmother
to whisk me far away."

Then suddenly, a tiny flea
popped up beside her seat.
It soon was joined by 3 more fleas
for filthy Fran to meet.

The faery flea, quite obviously
the leader of the pack,
said, "Fran, we're here to take you places
and to bring you back.
For sometimes, when you close your eyes,
and wish upon a star,
the faeries make your dreams come true,
no matter who you are."

"So we will be your Faery Fleas."
But Franny sighed, "Oh brother!
Who ever heard of Faery Fleas?
I wanted a Godmother."

"For you? A Faery Godmother?
Godmothers are too clean!
What Godmother could we send here?
How could we be that mean?
Fran dear, you better stick with us
because, you see, you give
a 4some like us Faery Fleas
a perfect place to live.

"And we can whisk you anywhere!
Oh, yeah, my name is Flo.
Now tell us all the places that you think
you'd like to go."

"4 Faery Fleas! You're just a tease. This can't be any fun."
But Frankie Flea piped up and said, "Let's try the Land of 1.

"The Land of 1 is lots of fun. I think you would adore it
'cause as the counting numbers go – well nothing comes before it.
1 Land has 1 of everything: 1 star, 1 moon, 1 sun.
And nothing there can multiply, because there's only 1."

The fleas jumped in a circle and consulted one another.
3 clapped their hands and did high-fives; all 3 ignored the other.

And Frankie said, "Yes!"
And Freddie said, "Yes!"
And Frieda said, "Yes!"
But Flo said, "No."

Then Freddie asked, "The Land of 2,
where everything's a pair?
2 shoes, 2 socks, 2 Goldilocks.
It's cozy. Let's go there."

And Frankie said, "Yes!"
And Freddie said, "Yes!"
And Frieda said, "Yes!"
But Flo said, "No."

"Well, we could see the land of 3," said Frieda in despair.
"Dimension wise, a 3 has size. Perhaps we should go there.
3 little pigs, 3 kittens and, of course, the 3 blind mice."
2 other fleas agreed with her. "The Land of 3 is nice!"

And Frankie said, "Yes!"
And Freddie said, "Yes!"
And Frieda said, "Yes!"
But Flo said, "No."

"We can't ignore the Land of 4," said funky Frankie Flea.
"4 Land is square. We'd like it there, with 2 + 2 to see.
"We'll all pick 4 leaf clovers and we'll ride a 4 wheeled bus.
4 Land would be our special land, because there's 4 of us!"

And Frankie said, "Yes!"
And Freddie said, "Yes!"
And Frieda said, "Yes!"
But Flo said, "No."

"Well let's jive to the Land of 5,
a gathering, grouping land.
We'll all count up five fingers
and we'll give ourselves a hand."

And Frankie said, "Yes!"
And Freddie said, "Yes!"
And Frieda said, "Yes!"
But Flo said, "No."

"A perfect fix! The Land of 6," said fussy Frieda Flea.
"6 is the perfect digit for a perfect flea like me.
And when Fran meets the critters there, I think she will discover they all have half a dozen legs. Is Fran an insect lover?"

And Frankie said, "Yes!"
And Freddie said, "Yes!"
And Frieda said, "Yes!"
But Flo said, "No."

"The earth has 7 continents
and also 7 seas.
The Land of 7 could be fun
for Franny and us Fleas."

And Frankie said, "Yes!"
And Freddie said, "Yes!"
And Frieda said, "Yes!"
But Flo said, "No."

Then Fred said, "Wait. The Land of 8,
the digit twisted round.
Since 8 is 2 x 2 x 2,
it's where the cubes are found.
With cubes of ice, and cubes for dice,
8 Land's a solid land,
where cubes and octahedrons
go hand in hand in hand."

And Frankie said, "Yes!"
And Freddie said, "Yes!"
And Frieda said, "Yes!"
But Flo said, "No."

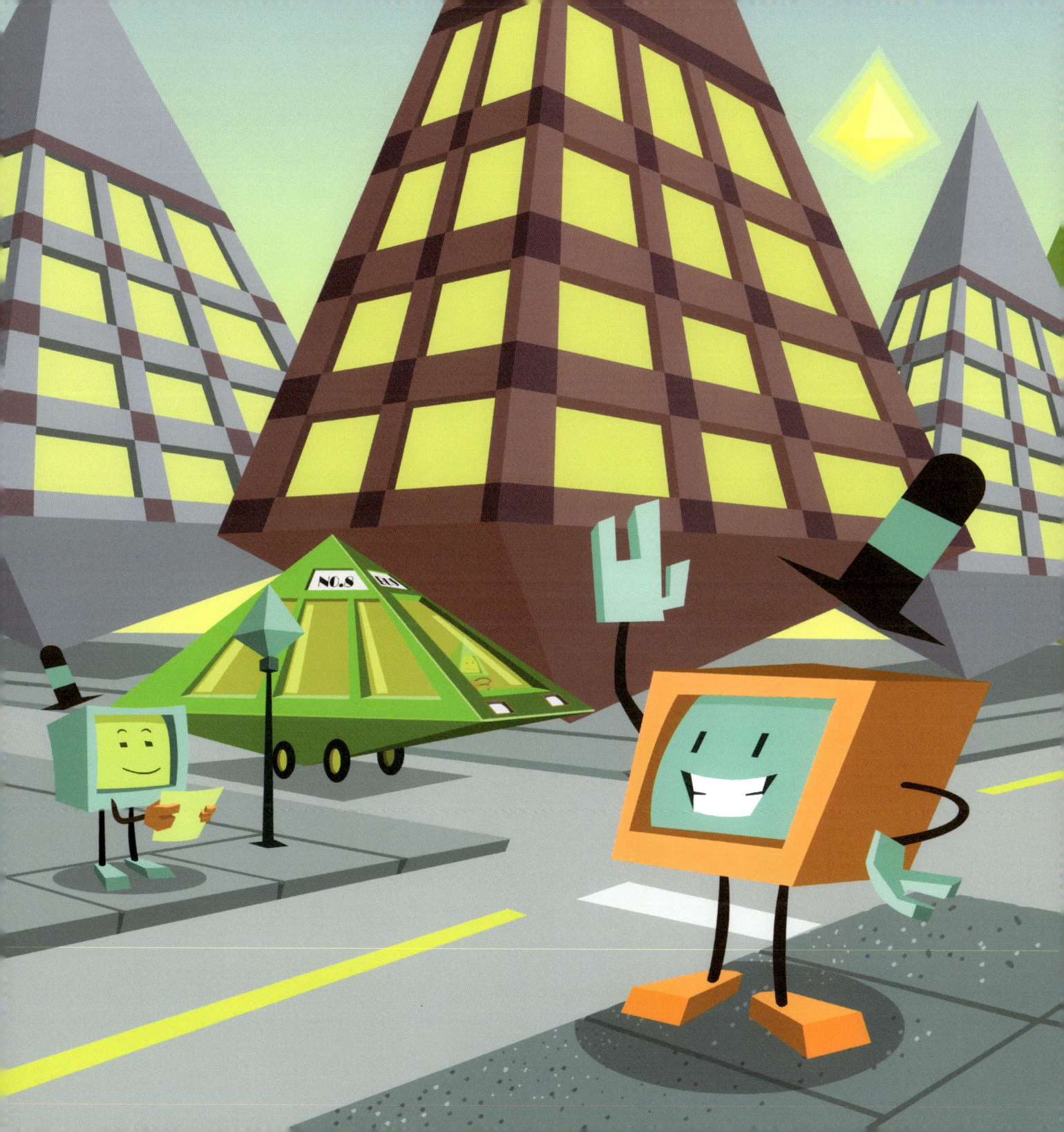

"OK, then fine! The Land of 9. It's square and 9 plays tricks:
sometimes a 9 will flip around and tell you it's a 6.
I'm not sure Fran will like it there," said Frankie, quite bereft,
"But as the lands of digits go, it's all that we have left."

And Frankie said, "Yes!"
And Freddie said, "Yes!"
And Frieda said, "Yes!"
But Flo said, "Whoa!"

"You 3 forgot a digit land, a land without a hero.
If we take Franny anyplace, we should take her to 0.
It's a great place for Franny. She could sit there by the hour
and never meet with anyone! She'd have no need to shower!"

Soon all the other faery fleas
agreed with leader Flo.
"An empty land for dirty kids,
wow, that's where Fran should go!"

And Frankie said, "Yes!"
And Freddie said, "Yes!"
And Frieda said, "Yes!"
And Flo said... "YES!"

But while the fleas were slapping backs
and shaking hands around,
Fran brushed them off the cushion
and they tumbled to the ground.

Fran jumped up from her messy chair
quite tired of fleas and math.
She grabbed some soap and towels
and she went to take a bath.

The End.

Meet the author: M.W. Penn

Marianne began her career writing software and designing software systems for AT&T, the University of Florida and the FDA. Software documentation and system manuals developed into a career in technical writing and numerous magazine articles in the field of architectural stone. A love of words and numbers and a strong belief that children should learn to appreciate both led Marianne to the interdisciplinary idea of presenting math in poetry. Marianne's first book, *Sidney the Silly Who Only Eats 6*, was awarded the 2008 Connecticut Press Club Communications Award for Best Children's Book of 2007. Her poetry appears in Highlights for Children and numerous anthologies including *A World of Stories* from Gumboot Books and *Caduceus* from the Yale Press. Marianne is an active conference presenter, and enjoys visiting schools to help spread her love of math and poetry to as many students as she can.

Gumboot Books titles by this author include:
Sidney the Silly Who Only Eats 6
Math & Poetry Fun With Sidney the Silly & Friends
The Number Tree (in A World of Stories collection)
Filthy Franny and the 4 Faery Fleas
ADDverse (volume 1)

Meet the illustrator: Mike Linton

Mike Linton is an animator and artist who currently resides in Vancouver, Canada. Mike has been working in animation for the last 15 years. He started working in hand drawn 2D animation and is now doing computer 3D. Never wanting to give up the pencil, he continues to draw and illustrate in his spare time. Thanks to Crystal and Gumboot Books, he has had the opportunity to try his hand at Children's book illustration.

Gumboot Books titles illustrated by this author include:
Filthy Franny and the 4 Faery Fleas
The Number Tree (in A World of Stories collection)

Gumboot Books is a socially and environmentally responsible company, and we measure our success by the impact we have on the lives and dreams of our authors and illustrators, the impact we have on the environment, and the ways in which we help to enrich the lives of everyone who reads our books.

If you'd like to see how else we are reducing our ecological footprint, and how we are supporting community numeracy and literacy projects, please visit us online.

www.gumbootbooks.com

ORDERING INFORMATION

All of our products are available through Amazon.com, Amazon.ca and other online retailers, directly from Gumboot Books online or call us toll free at 1-888-803-4861.

Quantity **discounts are available** on bulk purchases of this book for resale, educational purposes, subscription incentives, or fundraising initiatives.

For more information, or to place an order, please visit us online at **www.gumbootbooks.com** or call 1-888-803-4861 (toll-free from anywhere in North America).

LaVergne, TN USA
13 June 2010
185933LV00001B